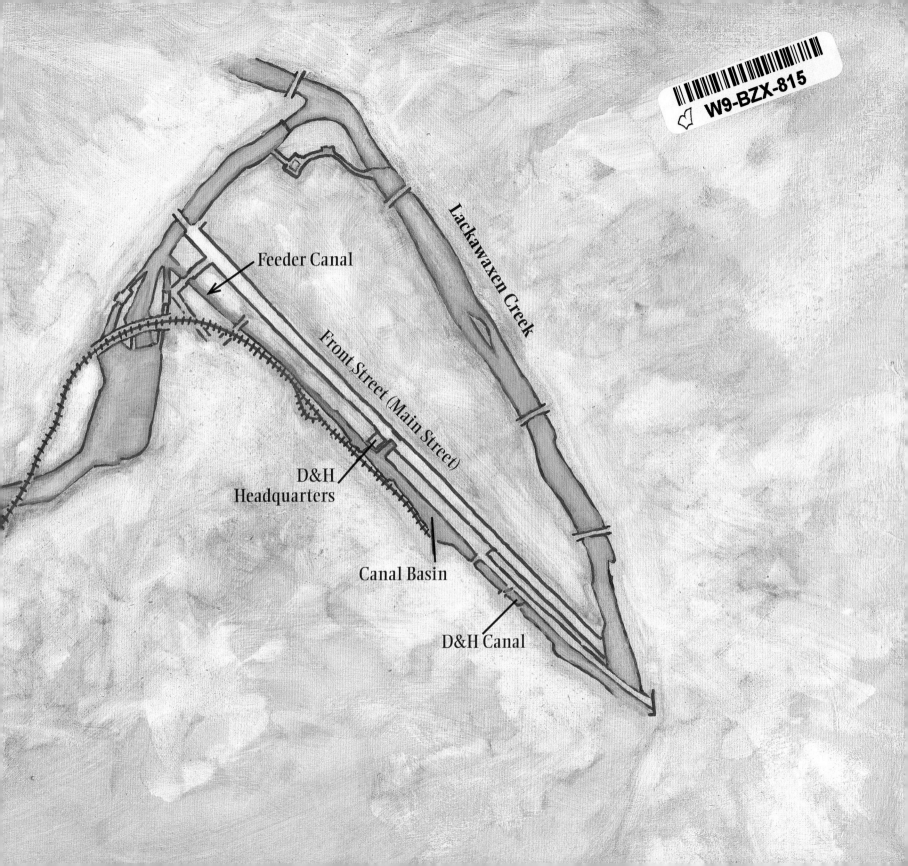

Feeder Canal

Lackawaxen Creek

Front Street (Main Street)

D&H
Headquarters

Canal Basin

D&H Canal

The STOURBRIDGE LION

America's First Locomotive

Karl Zimmermann

Illustrated by Steven Walker

BOYDS MILLS PRESS
HONESDALE, PENNSYLVANIA

Acknowledgements

The author and the illustrator wish to thank Jim Bader, Stan Pratt, Jim Shaughnessy, Sally Talaga, and the Wayne County Historical Society.

For information about permission to reproduce selections from this book,
please contact permissions@highlights.com.

Boyds Mills Press, Inc.
815 Church Street
Honesdale, Pennsylvania 18431
boydsmillspress.com
Printed in China

ISBN: 978-1-59078-859-2
Library of Congress Control Number: 2011939995

First edition
The text of this book is set in ITC Slimbach Book.
The illustrations are done in oils.

10 9 8 7 6 5 4 3 2 1

Another one for Lily

—KZ

To my wonderful wife, Evelyn, who keeps me going

—SW

They crisscross the country like a steel web, over two hundred thousand miles of them. From north to south and east to west, railroad tracks today carry passengers and freight all over the United States. But things were different in the early nineteenth century.

Back then, only a few miles of railroad track were in place, and the trains that ran on them were pulled by horses, not locomotives. Canals were becoming increasingly important to transportation.

In the 1820s and for many years after, most American homes were heated with coal. Anthracite, a hard coal that burned with little smoke or soot, was ideal for heating, and the best supply of anthracite lay under the hills of northeastern Pennsylvania.

To feed the hunger for coal, the Delaware and Hudson Canal was opened in 1828. Barges loaded with coal were pulled by horses or mules and traveled 108 miles from Honesdale in Pennsylvania to the Hudson River in New York.

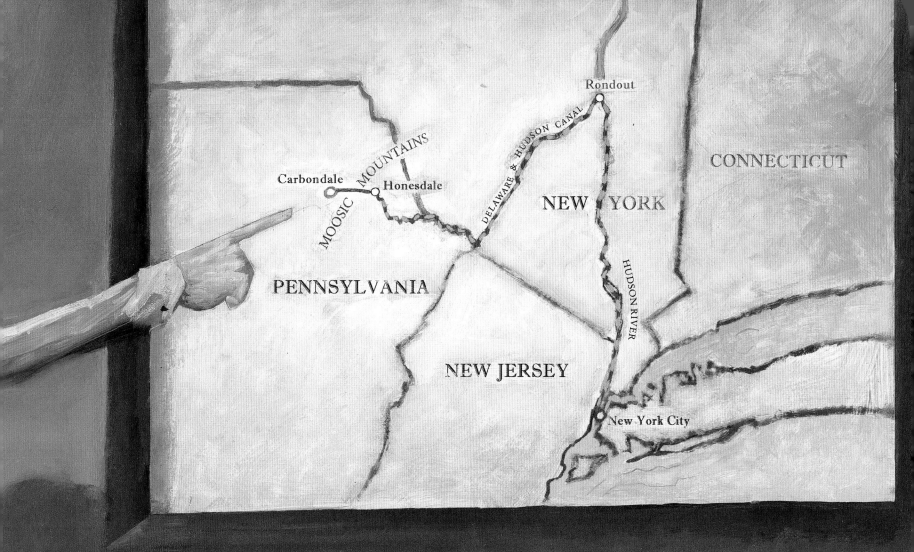

Honesdale was only sixteen miles from the coalfields, but the canal couldn't reach them. The Moosic Mountains stood in the way. The Delaware and Hudson Canal Company thought a railroad could bridge the gap. Trains could haul the coal up and over the mountains. So the company sent twenty-five-year-old Horatio Allen to England to purchase steam locomotives.

One of the steam locomotives that Allen purchased was built in the town of Stourbridge, England. When a worker painted a lion's head on the front of its boiler, the locomotive was named the *Stourbridge Lion*. It would become the first locomotive to operate on commercial rails in America.

Now that he had the *Stourbridge Lion* and his other locomotives, Horatio Allen sailed back to Pennsylvania. The *Lion* followed.

After arriving in New York City, the *Stourbridge Lion* traveled up the Hudson River by steamboat to a town called Rondout, where it was transferred to a D&H canalboat for the trip to Honesdale.

When the *Stourbridge Lion* arrived in Honesdale, Horatio Allen was there to greet it. Townspeople didn't know what to make of the contraption. They'd never seen anything like it. Some thought it was funny and laughed. Others thought the iron monster was scary. In any case, no one would join Allen on the first trial run. He'd be riding the *Lion* alone.

When the sun rose in Honesdale on August 8, 1829, Horatio Allen prepared for his history-making run. Townspeople were skeptical. Would this odd-looking beast stay on the rails? Would it plunge into the nearby creek? Would it break down?

Allen shoveled coal into the firebox. He opened the throttle. Amid swirls of smoke and clouds of steam, the *Stourbridge Lion* began to move. The crowd cheered as it watched the *Lion* gain speed. It swung across a high wooden trestle that curved over Lackawaxen Creek and then headed into the woods and out of sight. Would Horatio Allen make it back safely? Many in the crowd doubted it.

With Allen at the throttle, the *Stourbridge Lion* rocked and rolled over the flimsy track for three miles until it came to Seely's Mills, where Allen slowed the engine to a stop. Coming up was an overhead bridge. He could see that the bridge was too low for the *Lion*'s smokestack to pass underneath. Putting his locomotive in reverse, Horatio Allen chugged back to Honesdale.

The waiting crowd erupted into cheers, shouting and waving flags. Cannons boomed in celebration of the great event. Those on hand that day in Honesdale had seen for the first time ever in America a steam locomotive run on a real railroad.

The *Stourbridge Lion*'s only purpose was to haul coal that came over the mountains from the mines around Carbondale. A system of cables and pulleys, powered by stationary steam engines, hauled the coal on the uphill sections of the railroad. The cars traveled down the slopes propelled by their own weight, or gravity. The *Stourbridge Lion* and other locomotives would haul the coal on the level stretches of track to the head of the canal basin at Honesdale.

The railroad had been designed for locomotives weighing four tons. The *Stourbridge Lion* weighed almost twice that much. It was clear to Horatio Allen and others that the *Lion* would quickly tear up the wooden tracks.

That, it seemed, was the end of the *Stourbridge Lion*'s story. However, some people didn't forget the *Stourbridge Lion* and its importance as the first commercial steam locomotive in America.

After another forty years had passed, the boiler and other found parts were donated to the Smithsonian Institution in Washington, DC. There they were reassembled as best they could be for display in the hall of transportation. Today this reconstructed piece of the *Lion* is on loan to the Baltimore & Ohio Railroad Museum in Baltimore, Maryland.

With its canal long abandoned, the Delaware & Hudson Railway, now a major northeastern railroad, built an exact replica of the original *Stourbridge Lion* for Chicago's 1933 Century of Progress International Exposition.

Later the locomotive was displayed at the 1939 New York World's Fair. After that, it was given on permanent loan to the Wayne County Historical Society in northeastern Pennsylvania.

Today the *Stourbridge Lion* rests securely inside the society's museum in Honesdale, the scene of its triumphant run nearly two centuries ago.

More About the *Stourbridge Lion*

The *Stourbridge Lion* was one of the locomotives that Horatio Allen purchased in England. He bought one locomotive named the *Pride of Newcastle* from George Stephenson, who was already building a locomotive called the *Rocket*. This engine would be considered the world's first successful steam locomotive. Allen ordered three more locomotives from John Urpeth Rastrick of Stourbridge, including the *Stourbridge Lion*. The fate of the other two, the *Delaware* and the *Hudson*, both named for the canal company, remains unknown.

The *Pride of Newcastle*, renamed *America*, was the first of the D&H locomotives to cross the Atlantic Ocean to New York City. Since there were no tracks available, the locomotive was put up on blocks for a demonstration and its boiler was fired up. Though its driving wheels spun in the air, spectators were still thrilled to see for the first time ever such a steaming, smoking beast in action.

Though *America* joined the *Stourbridge Lion* on its journey up the Hudson River, it may never have made it to Honesdale. Some historians believe its boiler exploded and was destroyed, an incident that the D&H may have hushed up.

Early Steam Engines

The first steam locomotives came in many shapes and designs as builders tried to figure out what worked best. Steam engines heat water in their boilers to make steam. While some early locomotives had vertical boilers, the *Lion*'s boiler was horizontal, with a smokestack at its front end. It was powered by four driving wheels, each pair linked by "side rods."

Delaware and Hudson Gravity Railroad

The *Stourbridge Lion* ran on tracks that were very different from the steel highways of modern railroads. They were lengths of wood with thin strips of iron, called strap rail, screwed to their top. Horatio Allen had purchased this rail in England.

The canal company's chief engineer had designed the railroad for locomotives weighing four tons. The *Stourbridge Lion* weighed almost twice that much.

The *Lion* was meant to work on a railroad that was nothing like those we know today. This was a gravity railroad. The coal cars were pulled up the mountain slopes by ropes, and later, iron cables powered by stationary steam engines. The cars would then travel down the slopes propelled by their own weight—or gravity.

Mixed among the gravity railroad's eight inclined planes, or slopes, were three level stretches of track. It was on one of those levels that the *Stourbridge Lion* was expected to run.

Sources

Allen, Horatio. *The Railroad Era: The First Five Years of Its Development*. New York: 1884.

Barbe, Walter B., and Kurt A. Reed. *History of Wayne County, Pennsylvania (1798–1998)*. Honesdale, PA: Wayne County Historical Society, 1998.

Leslie, Vernon. *Honesdale and the Stourbridge Lions*. Honesdale, PA: Wayne County Historical Society, 1994.

Shaughnessy, Jim. *Delaware & Hudson: The History of an Important Railroad Whose Antecedent Was a Canal Network to Transport Coal*. Berkeley, CA: Howell-North Books, 1967.

Solomon, Brian. *Railroads of Pennsylvania: Your Guide to Pennsylvania's Historic Trains and Railway Sites*. Minneapolis, MN: Voyageur Press, 2008.

White, John H., Jr. *A History of the American Locomotive: Its Development, 1830-1880*. Mineola, NY: Dover Publications, 1980.

For more information about the *Stourbridge Lion*, please contact:

Wayne County Historical Society
P.O. Box 446, 810 Main Street
Honesdale, Pennsylvania 18431
Phone: (570) 253-3240
waynehistorypa.org
(website active at time of publication)

Pennsylvania

New York

D&H Gravity Railroad

Carbondale   Honesdale

Moosic Mountains

D&H Canal

DELAWARE & HUDSON CANAL

New Jersey